George Pinner of Wakefield

By
Robert Greene

ANODOS BOOKS
Candida Casa

Robert Greene (1558-1592)

Originally published in 1598
Editing, cover, and internal design by Alisdair MacNoravaich for Anodos Books.
Copyright © 2018 Anodos Books. All rights reserved.

Anodos Books
1c Kings Road
Whithorn
Newton Stewart
Dumfries & Galloway
DG8 8PP

Contents

DRAMATIS PERSONAE	1
ACT I.	3
ACT II.	13
ACT III.	25
ACT IV.	33
ACT V.	43
APPENDIX	51

DRAMATIS PERSONAE

EDWARD, King of England.
JAMES, King of Scotland.
EARL OF KENDAL.
EARL OF WARWICK.
LORD BONFIELD.
LORD HUMES.
SIR GILBERT ARMSTRONG.
SIR NICHOLAS MANNERING.
GEORGE-A-GREENE.
MUSGROVE.
CUDDY, his son.
NED-A-BARLEY.
GRIME.
ROBIN HOOD.
MUCH, the Miller's son.
SCARLET.
JENKIN, George-a-Greene's man.
WILY, George-a-Greene's boy.
JOHN.
Justice.
Townsmen, Shoemakers, Soldiers, Messengers, etc.
Jane-a-Barley
BETTRIS, daughter to Grime.
MAID MARIAN.

ACT I.

SCENE I.—*At Bradford.*

Enter the Earl of Kendal; *with him* Lord Bonfield, Sir Gilbert Armstrong, Sir Nicholas Mannering, *and* John.

Ken. Welcome to Bradford, martial gentlemen,
Lord Bonfield, and Sir Gilbert Armstrong both;
And all my troops, even to my basest groom,
Courage and welcome! for the day is ours.
Our cause is good, 'tis for the land's avail:
Then let us fight, and die for England's good.

All. We will, my lord.

Ken. As I am Henry Momford, Kendal's earl,
You honour me with this assent of yours;
And here upon my sword I make protest
For to relieve the poor or die myself.
And know, my lords, that James, the King of Scots,
Wars hard upon the borders of this land:
Here is his post.—Say, John Taylor, what news with King James?

John. War, my lord, [I] tell, and good news, I trow; for King Jamy vows to meet you the twenty-sixth of this month, God willing; marry, doth he, sir.

Ken. My friends, you see what we have to win.—
Well, John, commend me to King James, and tell him,
I will meet him the twenty-sixth of this month,
And all the rest; and so, farewell. [*Exit* John.
Bonfield, why stand'st thou as a man in dumps?
Courage! for, if I win, I'll make thee duke:
I, Henry Momford will be king myself;
And I will make thee Duke of Lancaster,
And Gilbert Armstrong Lord of Doncaster.

Bon. Nothing, my lord, makes me amaz'd at all,
But that our soldiers find our victuals scant.
We must make havoc of those country-swains;
For so will the rest tremble and be afraid,
And humbly send provision to your camp.

Arm. My Lord Bonfield gives good advice:
They make a scorn, and stand upon the king;
So what is brought is sent from them perforce;
Ask Mannering else.

Ken. What say'st thou, Mannering?

Man. Whenas I show'd your high commission,
They made this answer,
Only to send provision for your horses.

Ken. Well, hie thee to Wakefield, bid the town
To send me all provision that I want,
Lest I, like martial Tamburlaine, lay waste
Their bordering countries, and leaving none alive
That contradicts my commission.

Man. Let me alone;
My lord, I'll make them vail[1] their plumes;
For whatsoe'er he be, the proudest knight,
Justice, or other, that gainsay'th your word,
I'll clap him fast, to make the rest to fear.

Ken. Do so, Nick: hie thee thither presently,
And let us hear of thee again to-morrow.

Man. Will you not remove, my lord?

Ken. No, I will lie at Bradford all this night
And all the next.—Come, Bonfield, let us go,
And listen out some bonny lasses here. [*Exeunt.*

SCENE II.—*At Wakefield.*

Enter the Justice, Townsmen, George-a-Greene, *and* Sir Nicholas Mannering *with his commission.*

Jus. Master Mannering, stand aside, whilst we confer
What is best to do.—Townsmen of Wakefield,
The Earl of Kendal here hath sent for victuals;
And in aiding him we show ourselves no less
Than traitors to the king; therefore

---
[1] Lower.

Let me hear, townsmen, what is your consents.

First Towns. Even as you please, we are all content.

Jus. Then, Master Mannering, we are resolv'd—

Man. As how?

Jus. Marry, sir, thus.
We will send the Earl of Kendal no victuals,
Because he is a traitor to the king;
And in aiding him we show ourselves no less.

Man. Why, men of Wakefield, are you waxen mad,
That present danger cannot whet your wits,
Wisely to make provision of yourselves?
The earl is thirty thousand men strong in power,
And what town soever him resist,
He lays it flat and level with the ground.
Ye silly men, you seek your own decay:
Therefore send my lord such provision as he wants,
So he will spare your town,
And come no nearer Wakefield than he is.

Jus. Master Mannering, you have your answer; you may be gone.

Man. Well, Woodroffe, for so I guess is thy name,
I'll make thee curse thy overthwart denial;
And all that sit upon the bench this day shall rue
The hour they have withstood my lord's commission.

Jus. Do thy worst, we fear thee not.

Man. See you these seals? before you pass the town,
I will have all things my lord doth want,
In spite of you.

Geo. Proud dapper Jack, vail bonnet to the bench
That represents the person of the king;
Or, sirrah, I'll lay thy head before thy feet.

Man. Why, who art thou?

Geo. Why, I am George-a-Greene,
True liege-man to my king,
Who scorns that men of such esteem as these
Should brook the braves of any traitorous squire.
You of the bench, and you, my fellow-friends,
Neighbours, we subjects all unto the king;
We are English born, and therefore Edward's friends.
Vow'd unto him even in our mothers' womb,
Our minds to God, our hearts unto our king:
Our wealth, our homage, and our carcases,
Be all King Edward's. Then, sirrah, we
Have nothing left for traitors, but our swords,
Whetted to bathe them in your bloods, and die
'Gainst you, before we send you any victuals.

Jus. Well spoken, George-a-Greene!

First Towns. Pray let George-a-Greene speak for us.

Geo. Sirrah, you get no victuals here,
Not if a hoof of beef would save your lives.

Man. Fellow, I stand amaz'd at thy presumption.
Why, what art thou that dar'st gainsay my lord,
Knowing his mighty puissance and his stroke?
Why, my friend, I come not barely of myself;
For, see, I have a large commission.

Geo. Let me see it, sirrah [*Takes the commission*].
Whose seals be these?

Man. This is the Earl of Kendal's seal-at-arms;
This Lord Charnel Bonfield's;
And this Sir Gilbert Armstrong's.

Geo. I tell thee, sirrah, did good King Edward's son
Seal a commission 'gainst the king his father,
Thus would I tear it in despite of him,
[*Tears the commission.*
Being traitor to my sovereign.

Man. What, hast thou torn my lord's commission?
Thou shalt rue it, and so shall all Wakefield.

Geo. What, are you in choler? I will give you pills
To cool your stomach. Seest thou these seals?
Now, by my father's soul,
Which was a yeoman when he was alive,
Eat them, or eat my dagger's point, proud squire.

Man. But thou dost but jest, I hope.

Geo. Sure that shall you see before we two part.

Man. Well, an there be no remedy, so, George:
[*Swallows one of the seals.*
One is gone; I pray thee, no more now.

Geo. O, sir, if one be good, the others cannot hurt.
[MANNERING *swallows the other two seals.*
So, sir; now you may go tell the Earl of Kendal,
Although I have rent his large commission,
Yet of courtesy I have sent all his seals
Back again by you.

Man. Well, sir, I will do your errand. [*Exit.*

Geo. Now let him tell his lord that he hath spoke
With George-a-Greene,
Hight Pinner of merry Wakefield town,
That hath physic for a fool,
Pills for a traitor that doth wrong his sovereign.
Are you content with this that I have done?

Jus. Ay, content, George;
For highly hast thou honour'd Wakefield town
In cutting off proud Mannering so short.
Come, thou shalt be my welcome guest to-day;
For well thou hast deserv'd reward and favour.
[*Exeunt.*

SCENE III.—*In Westmoreland.*

Enter MUSGROVE *and* CUDDY.

Cud. Now, gentle father, list unto thy son,
And for my mother's love,

That erst was blithe and bonny in thine eye,
Grant one petition that I shall demand.

Mus. What is that, my Cuddy?

Cud. Father, you know the ancient enmity of late
Between the Musgroves and the wily Scots,
Whereof they have oath
Not to leave one alive that strides a lance.
O father, you are old, and, waning, age unto the grave:
Old William Musgrove, which whilom was thought
The bravest horseman in all Westmoreland,
Is weak, and forc'd to stay his arm upon a staff,
That erst could wield a lance.
Then, gentle father, resign the hold to me;
Give arms to youth, and honour unto age.

Mus. Avaunt, false-hearted boy! my joints do quake
Even with anguish of thy very words.
Hath William Musgrove seen an hundred years?
Have I been fear'd and dreaded of the Scots,
That, when they heard my name in any road,[2]
They fled away, and posted thence amain,
And shall I die with shame now in mine age?
No, Cuddy, no: thus resolve I,
Here have I liv'd, and here will Musgrove die.
[*Exeunt.*

SCENE IV.—*At Bradford.*

Enter Lord Bonfield, Sir Gilbert Armstrong, Grime, *and* Bettris.

Bon. Now, gentle Grime, God-a-mercy for our good cheer;
Our fare was royal, and our welcome great:
And sith so kindly thou hast entertain'd us,
If we return with happy victory,
We will deal as friendly with thee in recompense.

Grime. Your welcome was but duty, gentle lord;
For wherefore have we given us our wealth,
But to make our betters welcome when they come?
[*Aside*]. O, this goes hard when traitors must be flatter'd!

_____
[2] Inroad.

But life is sweet, and I cannot withstand it:
God, I hope, will revenge the quarrel of my king.

Arm. What said you, Grime?

Grime. I say, Sir Gilbert, looking on my daughter,
I curse the hour that e'er I got the girl;
For, sir, she may have many wealthy suitors,
And yet she disdains them all,
To have poor George-a-Greene unto her husband.

Bon. On that, good Grime, I am talking with thy daughter;
But she, in quirks and quiddities of love,
Sets me to school, she is so over-wise.—
But, gentle girl, if thou wilt forsake the Pinner
And be my love, I will advance thee high;
To dignify those hairs of amber hue,
I'll grace them with a chaplet made of pearl,
Set with choice rubies, sparks, and diamonds,
Planted upon a velvet hood, to hide that head
Wherein two sapphires burn like sparkling fire:
This will I do, fair Bettris, and far more,
If thou wilt love the Lord of Doncaster.

Bet. Heigh-ho! my heart is in a higher place,
Perhaps on the earl, if that be he.
See where he comes, or angry, or in love,
For why his colour looketh discontent.

Enter the EARL OF KENDAL *and* SIR NICHOLAS MANNERING.

Ken. Come, Nick, follow me.

Bon. How now, my lord! what news?

Ken. Such news, Bonfield, as will make thee laugh,
And fret thy fill, to hear how Nick was us'd.
Why, the Justices stand on their terms:
Nick, as you know, is haughty in his words;
He laid the law unto the Justices
With threatening braves, that one look'd on another,
Ready to stoop; but that a churl came in,
One George-a-Greene, the Pinner of the town,

And with his dagger drawn laid hands on Nick,
And by no beggars swore that we were traitors,
Rent our commission, and upon a brave
Made Nick to eat the seals or brook the stab:
Poor Mannering, afraid, came posting hither straight.

Bet. O lovely George, fortune be still thy friend!
And as thy thoughts be high, so be thy mind
In all accords, even to thy heart's desire!

Bon. What says fair Bettris?

Grime. My lord, she is praying for George-a-Greene:
He is the man, and she will none but him.

Bon. But him! why, look on me, my girl:
Thou know'st, that yesternight I courted thee,
And swore at my return to wed with thee.
Then tell me, love, shall I have all thy fair?

Bet. I care not for earl, nor yet for knight,
Nor baron that is so bold;
For George-a-Greene, the merry Pinner,
He hath my heart in hold.[3]

Bon. Bootless, my lord, are many vain replies:
Let us hie us to Wakefield, and send her the Pinner's head.

Ken. It shall be so.—Grime, gramercy,
Shut up thy daughter, bridle her affects;[4]
Let me not miss her when I make return;
Therefore look to her, as to thy life, good Grime.

Grime. I warrant you, my lord.

Ken. And, Bettris,
Leave a base Pinner, for to love an earl.
[*Exeunt* Grime *and* Bettris.
Fain would I see this Pinner George-a-Greene.
It shall be thus:
Nick Mannering shall lead on the battle,

---

[3]In ballad style, though not found in the ballad "The Jolly Pinder of Wakefield."
[4]Affections.

And we three will go to Wakefield in some disguise:
But howsoever, I'll have his head to-day. [*Exeunt.*

ACT II.

SCENE I.—*Before* Sir John-a-Barley's *Castle*.

Enter James, King of Scots, Lord Humes, *with* Soldiers, *and* John.

K. James. Why, Johnny, then the Earl of Kendal is blithe,
And hath brave men that troop along with him?

John. Ay, marry, my liege,
And hath good men that come along with him,
And vows to meet you at Scrasblesea, God willing.

K. James. If good Saint Andrew lend King Jamy leave,
I will be with him at the 'pointed day.

Enter Ned.

But, soft!—Whose pretty boy art thou?

Ned. Sir, I am son unto Sir John-a-Barley,
Eldest, and all that e'er my mother had;
Edward my name.

K. James. And whither art thou going, pretty Ned?

Ned. To seek some birds, and kill them, if I can:
And now my schoolmaster is also gone,
So have I liberty to ply my bow;
For when he comes, I stir not from my book.

K. James. Lord Humes, but mark the visage of this child:
By him I guess the beauty of his mother;
None but Leda could breed Helena.—
Tell me, Ned, who is within with thy mother?

Ned. Naught but herself and household servants, sir:
If you would speak with her, knock at this gate.

K. James. Johnny, knock at that gate.
[John *knocks at the gate.*

Enter Jane-a-Barley *upon the walls.*

Jane. O, I'm betray'd! What multitudes be these?

K. James. Fear not, fair Jane, for all these men are mine,
And all thy friends, if thou be friend to me:
I am thy lover, James the King of Scots,
That oft have su'd and woo'd with many letters,
Painting my outward passions with my pen,
Whenas my inward soul did bleed for woe.
Little regard was given to my suit;
But haply thy husband's presence wrought it:
Therefore, sweet Jane, I fitted me to time,
And, hearing that thy husband was from home,
Am come to crave what long I have desir'd.

Ned. Nay, soft you, sir! you get no entrance here,
That seek to wrong Sir John-a-Barley so,
And offer such dishonour to my mother.

K. James. Why, what dishonour, Ned?

Ned. Though young,
Yet often have I heard my father say,
No greater wrong than to be made cuckold.
Were I of age, or were my body strong,
Were he ten kings, I would shoot him to the heart
That should attempt to give Sir John the horn.—
Mother, let him not come in:
I will go lie at Jocky Miller's house.

K. James. Stay him.

Jane. Ay, well said; Ned, thou hast given the king his answer;
For were the ghost of Cæsar on the earth,
Wrapp'd in the wonted glory of his honour,
He should not make me wrong my husband so.
But good King James is pleasant, as I guess,
And means to try what humour I am in;
Else would he never have brought an host of men,
To have them witness of his Scottish lust.

K. James. Jane, in faith, Jane,—

Jane. Never reply,

For I protest by the highest holy God,
That doometh just revenge for things amiss,
King James, of all men, shall not have my love.

K. James. Then list to me: Saint Andrew be my boot,
But I'll raze thy castle to the very ground,
Unless thou open the gate, and let me in.

Jane. I fear thee not, King Jamy: do thy worst.
This castle is too strong for thee to scale;
Besides, to-morrow will Sir John come home.

K. James. Well, Jane, since thou disdain'st King James's love,
I'll draw thee on with sharp and deep extremes;
For, by my father's soul, this brat of thine
Shall perish here before thine eyes,
Unless thou open the gate, and let me in.

Jane. O deep extremes! my heart begins to break:
My little Ned looks pale for fear.—
Cheer thee, my boy, I will do much for thee.

Ned. But not so much as to dishonour me.

Jane. An if thou diest, I cannot live, sweet Ned.

Ned. Then die with honour, mother, dying chaste.

Jane. I am armed:
My husband's love, his honour, and his fame,
Join[5] victory by virtue. Now, King James,
If mother's tears cannot allay thine ire,
Then butcher him, for I will never yield:
The son shall die before I wrong the father.

K. James. Why, then, he dies.

     Alarum within. Enter a Messenger.

Mess. My lord, Musgrove is at hand.

K. James. Who, Musgrove? The devil he is! Come, my horse!

---
[5] For "enjoin."

[*Exeunt.*

SCENE II.—*The Same.*

Enter Musgrove *with* King James *prisoner*; Jane-a-Barley *on the walls.*

Mus. Now, King James, thou art my prisoner.

K. James. Not thine, but fortune's prisoner.

Enter Cuddy.

Cud. Father, the field is ours: their colours we have seiz'd,
And Humes is slain; I slew him hand to hand.

Mus. God and Saint George!

Cud. O father, I am sore athirst!

Jane. Come in, young Cuddy, come and drink thy fill:
Bring in King Jamy with you as a guest;
For all this broil was 'cause he could not enter.
[*Exit above.—Exeunt below, the others.*

SCENE III.—*At Wakefield.*

Enter George-a-Greene.

Geo. The sweet content of men that live in love
Breeds fretting humours in a restless mind;
And fancy, being check'd by fortune's spite,
Grows too impatient in her sweet desires;
Sweet to those men whom love leads on to bliss,
But sour to me whose hap is still amiss.

Enter Jenkin.

Jen. Marry, amen, sir.

Geo. Sir, what do you cry "amen" at?

Jen. Why, did not you talk of love?

Geo. How do you know that?

Jen. Well, though I say it that should not say it, there are few fellows in our parish so nettled with love as I have been of late.

Geo. Sirrah, I thought no less, when the other morning you rose so early to go to your wenches. Sir, I had thought you had gone about my honest business.

Jen. Trow, you have hit it; for, master, be it known to you, there is some good-will betwixt Madge the souce-wife[6] and I; marry, she hath another lover.

Geo. Can'st thou brook any rivals in thy love?

Jen. A rider! no, he is a sow-gelder and goes afoot. But Madge 'pointed to meet me in your wheat-close.

Geo. Well, did she meet you there?

Jen. Never make question of that. And first I saluted her with a green gown, and after fell as hard a-wooing as if the priest had been at our backs to have married us.

Geo. What, did she grant?

Jen. Did she grant! never make question of that. And she gave me a shirt-collar wrought over with no counterfeit stuff.

Geo. What, was it gold?

Jen. Nay, 'twas better than gold.

Geo. What was it?

Jen. Right Coventry blue. We had no sooner come there but wot you who came by?

Geo. No: who?

Jen. Clim the sow-gelder.

Geo. Came he by?

Jen. He spied Madge and I sit together: he leapt from his horse, laid his hand on his dagger, and began to swear. Now I seeing he had a dagger, and I nothing but this twig in my hand, I gave him fair words and said nothing. He comes to me, and takes me by the bosom. "You whoreson slave," said he, "hold my horse, and look he take no cold in his feet." "No, marry, shall he, sir," quoth I; "I'll lay my cloak underneath him." I took my cloak, spread it all along, and his horse on the midst of it.

---
[6] A woman who sells "souce" or brine for pickling.

Geo. Thou clown, didst thou set his horse upon thy cloak?

Jen. Ay, but mark how I served him. Madge and he was no sooner gone down into the ditch, but I plucked out my knife, cut four holes in my cloak, and made his horse stand on the bare ground.

Geo. 'Twas well done. Now, sir, go and survey my fields: if you find any cattle in the corn, to pound with them.

Jen. And if I find any in the pound, I shall turn them out. [*Exit.*

Enter the EARL OF KENDAL, LORD BONFIELD, SIR GILBERT ARMSTRONG, *all disguised, with a train of men.*

Ken. Now we have put the horses in the corn,
Let us stand in some corner for to hear
What braving terms the Pinner will breathe
When he spies our horses in the corn.
[*Retires with the others.*

Re-enter JENKIN *blowing his horn.*

Jen. O master, where are you? we have a prize.

Geo. A prize! what is it?

Jen. Three goodly horses in our wheat-close.

Geo. Three horses in our wheat-close! whose be they?

Jen. Marry, that's a riddle to me; but they are there; velvet[7] horses, and I never saw such horses before. As my duty was, I put off my cap, and said as followeth: "My masters, what do you make in our close?" One of them, hearing me ask what he made there, held up his head and neighed, and after his manner laughed as heartily as if a mare had been tied to his girdle. "My masters," said I, "it is no laughing matter; for, if my master take you here, you go as round as a top to the pound." Another untoward jade, hearing me threaten him to the pound and to tell you of them, cast up both his heels, and let such a monstrous great fart, that was as much as in his language to say, "A fart for the pound, and a fart for George-a-Greene!" Now I, hearing this, put on my cap, blew my horn, called them all jades, and came to tell you.

Geo. Now, sir, go and drive me those three horses to the pound.

---

[7]"Allusions to velvet as being costly, fine, and luxurious are very common in the Elizabethan writers."—Collins.

Jen. Do you hear? I were best to take a constable with me.

Geo. Why so?

Jen. Why, they, being gentlemen's horses, may stand on their reputation, and will not obey me.

Geo. Go, do as I bid you, sir.

Jen. Well, I may go.

> *The* Earl of Kendal, Lord Bonfield, *and* Sir Gilbert Armstrong *come forward.*

Ken. Whither away, sir?

Jen. Whither away! I am going to put the horses in the pound.

Ken. Sirrah, those three horses belong to us,
And we put them in,
And they must tarry there and eat their fill.

Jen. Stay, I will go tell my master.—Hear you, master? we have another prize: those three horses be in your wheat-close still, and here be three geldings more.

Geo. What be these?

Jen. These are the masters of the horses.

Geo. Now, gentlemen (I know not your degrees,
But more you cannot be, unless you be kings,)
Why wrong you us of Wakefield with your horses?
I am the Pinner, and, before you pass,
You shall make good the trespass they have done.

Ken. Peace, saucy mate, prate not to us:
I tell thee, Pinner, we are gentlemen.

Geo. Why, sir, so may I, sir, although I give no arms.

Ken. Thou! how art thou a gentleman?

Jen. And such is my master, and he may give as good arms as ever your great-grandfather could give.

Ken. Pray thee, let me hear how.

Jen. Marry, my master may give for his arms the picture of April in a green jerkin, with a rook on one fist and an horn on the other: but my master gives his arms the wrong way, for he gives the horn on his fist; and your grandfather, because he would not lose his arms, wears the horn on his own head.

Ken. Well, Pinner, sith our horses be in,
In spite of thee they now shall feed their fill,
And eat until our leisures serve to go.

Geo. Now, by my father's soul,
Were good King Edward's horses in the corn,
They shall amend the scath, or kiss the pound;
Much more yours, sir, whatsoe'er you be.

Ken. Why, man, thou knowest not us:
We do belong to Henry Momford, Earl of Kendal;
Men that, before a month be full expir'd,
Will be King Edward's betters in the land.

Geo. King Edward's betters! Rebel, thou liest!
[*Strikes him.*

Bon. Villain, what hast thou done? thou hast struck an earl.

Geo. Why, what care I? a poor man that is true,
Is better than an earl, if he be false.
Traitors reap no better favours at my hands.

Ken. Ay, so methinks; but thou shalt dear aby[8] this blow.—
Now or never lay hold on the Pinner!

All the train comes forward.

Geo. Stay, my lords, let us parley on these broils:
Not Hercules against two, the proverb is,
Nor I against so great a multitude.—
[*Aside*]. Had not your troops come marching as they did,
I would have stopt your passage unto London:
But now I'll fly to secret policy.

Ken. What dost thou murmur, George?

---

[8]Pay the penalty for.

Geo. Marry, this, my lord; I muse,
If thou be Henry Momford, Kendal's earl,
That thou wilt do poor George-a-Greene this wrong,
Ever to match me with a troop of men.

Ken Why dost thou strike me, then?

Geo. Why, my lord, measure me but by yourself:
Had you a man had serv'd you long,
And heard your foe misuse you behind your back,
And would not draw his sword in your defence,
You would cashier him.
Much more, King Edward is my king:
And before I'll hear him so wrong'd,
I'll die within this place,
And maintain good whatsoever I have said.
And, if I speak not reason in this case,
What I have said I'll maintain in this place.

Bon. A pardon, my lord, for this Pinner;
For, trust me, he speaketh like a man of worth.

Ken. Well, George, wilt thou leave Wakefield and wend with me,
I'll freely put up all and pardon thee.

Geo. Ay, my lord, considering me one thing,
You will leave these arms, and follow your good king.

Ken. Why, George, I rise not against King Edward,
But for the poor that is oppress'd by wrong;
And, if King Edward will redress the same,
I will not offer him disparagement,
But otherwise; and so let this suffice.
Thou hear'st the reason why I rise in arms:
Now, wilt thou leave Wakefield and wend with me,
I'll make thee captain of a hardy band,
And, when I have my will, dub thee a knight.

Geo. Why, my lord, have you any hope to win?

Ken. Why, there is a prophecy doth say,
That King James and I shall meet at London,

And make the king vail bonnet to us both.

Geo. If this were true, my lord, this were a mighty reason.

Ken. Why, it is a miraculous prophecy, and cannot fail.

Geo. Well, my lord, you have almost turned me.—
Jenkin, come hither.

Jen. Sir?

Geo. Go your ways home, sir,
And drive me those three horses home unto my house,
And pour them down a bushel of good oats.

Jen. Well, I will.—[*Aside*]. Must I give these scurvy horses oats?
[*Exit.*

Geo. Will it please you to command your train aside?

Ken. Stand aside. [*The train retires.*

Geo. Now list to me:
Here in a wood, not far from hence,
There dwells an old man in a cave alone,
That can foretell what fortunes shall befall you,
For he is greatly skilful in magic art.
Go you three to him early in the morning,
And question him: if he says good,
Why, then, my lord, I am the foremost man
Who will march up with your camp to London.

Ken. George, thou honourest me in this. But where shall we find him out?

Geo. My man shall conduct you to the place;
But, good my lord, tell me true what the wise man saith.

Ken. That will I, as I am Earl of Kendal.

Geo. Why, then, to honour George-a-Greene the more,
Vouchsafe a piece of beef at my poor house;
You shall have wafer-cakes your fill,

A piece of beef hung up since Martlemas:
If that like you not, take what you bring, for me.

Ken. Gramercies, George. [*Exeunt.*

ACT III.

SCENE I.—*Before* Grime's *house in Bradford.*

Enter George-a-Greene's *boy* Wily, *disguised as a woman.*

Wily. O, what is love! it is some mighty power,
Else could it never conquer George-a-Greene.
Here dwells a churl that keeps away his love:
I know the worst, an if I be espied,
'Tis but a beating; and if I by this means
Can get fair Bettris forth her father's door,
It is enough.
Venus, for me, of all the gods alone,
Be aiding to my wily enterprise! [*Knocks at the door.*

Enter Grime *as from the house.*

Grime. How now! who knocks there? what would you have?
From whence came you? where do you dwell?

Wily. I am, forsooth, a sempster's maid hard by,
That hath brought work home to your daughter.

Grime. Nay, are you not
Some crafty quean that comes from George-a-Greene,
That rascal, with some letters to my daughter?
I will have you search'd.

Wily. Alas, sir, it is Hebrew unto me,
To tell me of George-a-Greene or any other!
Search me, good sir, and if you find a letter
About me, let me have the punishment that's due.

Grime. Why are you muffled? I like you the worse for that.

Wily. I am not, sir, asham'd to show my face;
Yet loth I am my cheeks should take the air:
Not that I'm chary of my beauty's hue,
But that I'm troubled with the toothache sore.
[*Unmuffles.*

Grime. [*aside*]. A pretty wench, of smiling countenance!
Old men can like, although they cannot love;

Ay, and love, though not so brief as young men can.—
Well, go in, my wench, and speak with my daughter.
[*Exit* Wily *into the house.*
I wonder much at the Earl of Kendal,
Being a mighty man, as still he is,
Yet for to be a traitor to his king,
Is more than God or man will well allow.
But what a fool am I to talk of him!
My mind is more here of the pretty lass.
Had she brought some forty pounds to town,
I could be content to make her my wife:
Yet I have heard it in a proverb said,
He that is old and marries with a lass,
Lies but at home, and proves himself an ass.

Enter, from the house, Bettris *in* Wily's *apparel.*

How now, my wench! how is't? what, not a word?—
Alas, poor soul, the toothache plagues her sore.—
Well, my wench,
Here is an angel for to buy thee pins, [*Gives money.*
And I pray thee use mine house;
The oftener, the more welcome: farewell. [*Exit.*

Bet. O blessèd love, and blessèd fortune both!
But, Bettris, stand not here to talk of love,
But hie thee straight unto thy George-a-Greene:
Never went roebuck swifter on the downs
Than I will trip it till I see my George. [*Exit.*

SCENE II.—*A Wood near Wakefield.*

Enter the Earl of Kendal, Lord Bonfield, Sir Gilbert Armstrong, *and* Jenkin.

Ken. Come away, Jenkin.

Jen. Come, here is his house. [*Knocks at the door.*]—Where be you, ho?

Geo. [*within*]. Who knocks there?

Ken. Here are two or three poor men, father, would speak with you.

Geo. [*within*]. Pray, give your man leave to lead me forth.

Ken. Go, Jenkin, fetch him forth. [Jenkin *leads forth* George-a-Greene *disguised.*

Jen. Come, old man.

Ken. Father, here are three poor men come to question thee
A word in secret that concerns their lives.

Geo. Say on, my sons.

Ken. Father, I am sure you hear the news, how that
The Earl of Kendal wars against the king.
Now, father, we three are gentlemen by birth,
But younger brethren that want revenues,
And for the hope we have to be preferr'd,
If that we knew that we shall win,
We will march with him: if not,
We will not march a foot to London more.
Therefore, good father, tell us what shall happen,
Whether the king or the Earl of Kendal shall win.

Geo. The king, my son.

Ken. Art thou sure of that?

Geo. Ay, as sure as thou art Henry Momford,
The one Lord Bonfield, the other Sir Gilbert [Armstrong].

Ken. Why, this is wondrous, being blind of sight,
His deep perceiverance should be such to know us.

Arm. Magic is mighty and foretelleth great matters.—
Indeed, father, here is the earl come to see thee,
And therefore, good father, fable not with him.

Geo. Welcome is the earl to my poor cell,
And so are you, my lords; but let me counsel you
To leave these wars against your king, and live in quiet.

Ken. Father, we come not for advice in war,
But to know whether we shall win or leese.[9]

Geo. Lose, gentle lords, but not by good King Edward;

---
[9]Lose.

A baser man shall give you all the foil.

Ken. Ay, marry, father, what man is that?

Geo. Poor George-a-Greene, the Pinner.

Ken. What shall he?

Geo. Pull all your plumes, and sore dishonour you.

Ken. He! as how?

Geo. Nay, the end tries all; but so it will fall out.

Ken. But so it shall not, by my honour Christ.
I'll raise my camp, and fire Wakefield town,
And take that servile Pinner George-a-Greene,
And butcher him before King Edward's face.

Geo. Good my lord, be not offended,
For I speak no more than art reveals to me:
And for greater proof,
Give your man leave to fetch me my staff.

Ken. Jenkin, fetch him his walking-staff.

Jen. [*giving it*]. Here is your walking-staff.

Geo. I'll prove it good upon your carcases;
A wiser wizard never met you yet,
Nor one that better could foredoom your fall.
Now I have singled you here alone,
I care not though you be three to one.

Ken. Villain, hast thou betray'd us?

Geo. Momford, thou liest, ne'er was I traitor yet;
Only devis'd this guile to draw you on
For to be combatants.
Now conquer me, and then march on to London:
It shall go hard but I will hold you task.

Arm. Come, my lord, cheerly, I'll kill him hand to hand.

Ken. A thousand pound to him that strikes that stroke!

Geo. Then give it me, for I will have the first.
[*Here they fight;* George *kills* Sir Gilbert Armstrong, *and takes the other two prisoners.*

Bon. Stay, George, we do appeal.

Geo. To whom?

Bon. Why, to the king:
For rather had we bide what he appoints,
Then here be murder'd by a servile groom.

Ken. What wilt thou do with us?

Geo. Even as Lord Bonfield wish'd,
You shall unto the king: and, for that purpose,
See where the Justice is plac'd.

Enter Justice.

Jus. Now, my Lord of Kendal, where be all your threats?
Even as the cause, so is the combat fallen,
Else one could never have conquer'd three.

Ken. I pray thee, Woodroffe, do not twit me;
If I have faulted, I must make amends.

Geo. Master Woodroffe, here is not a place for many words:
I beseech ye, sir, discharge all his soldiers,
That every man may go home unto his own house.

Jus. It shall be so. What wilt thou do, George?

Geo. Master Woodroffe, look to your charge;
Leave me to myself.

Jus. Come, my lords.
[*Exeunt all except* George.

SCENE III.—*A Wood near Wakefield.*

GEORGE-A-GREENE *discovered.*[10]

Geo. Here sit thou, George, wearing a willow wreath,
As one despairing of thy beauteous love:
Fie, George! no more;
Pine not away for that which cannot be.
I cannot joy in any earthly bliss,
So long as I do want my Bettris.

Enter JENKIN.

Jen. Who see a master of mine?

Geo. How now, sirrah! whither away?

Jen, Whither away! why, who do you take me to be?

Geo. Why, Jenkin, my man.

Jen. I was so once indeed, but now the case is altered.

Geo. I pray thee, as how?

Jen. Were not you a fortune-teller to-day?

Geo. Well, what of that?

Jen. So sure am I become a juggler. What will you say if I juggle your sweetheart?

Geo. Peace, prating losel! her jealous father
Doth wait o'er her with such suspicious eyes,
That, if a man but dally by her feet,
He thinks it straight a witch to charm his daughter.

Jen. Well, what will you give me, if I bring her hither?

Geo. A suit of green, and twenty crowns besides.

Jen. Well, by your leave, give me room. You must give me something that you have lately worn.

Geo. Here is a gown, will that serve you?
[*Gives gown.*

Jen. Ay, this will serve me. Keep out of my circle, lest you be torn in

---

[10]Here the scene may be supposed to have changed, although George has not left the stage. In the quarto the scene runs on without break.

pieces by she-devils.—Mistress Bettris, once, twice, thrice!
[JENKIN *throws the gown in, and* BETTRIS *comes out.*[11]
O, is this no cunning?

Geo. Is this my love, or is it but her shadow?

Jen. Ay, this is the shadow, but here is the substance.

Geo. Tell me, sweet love, what good fortune brought thee hither?
For one it was that favour'd George-a-Greene.

Bet. Both love and fortune brought me to my George,
In whose sweet sight is all my heart's content.

Geo. Tell me, sweet love, how cam'st thou from thy father's?

Bet. A willing mind hath many slips in love:
It was not I, but Wily, thy sweet boy.

Geo. And where is Wily now?

Bet. In my apparel, in my chamber still.

Geo. Jenkin, come hither: go to Bradford,
And listen out your fellow Wily.—
Come, Bettris, let us in,
And in my cottage we will sit and talk.
[*Exeunt.*

---

[11] Through a door at the back of the stage.

ACT IV.

SCENE I.—*Camp of* King Edward.

Enter King Edward, James, King of Scots, Lord Warwick, Cuddy, *and* Train.

K. Edw. Brother of Scotland, I do hold it hard,
Seeing a league of truce was late confirm'd
'Twixt you and me, without displeasure offer'd
You should make such invasion in my land.
The vows of kings should be as oracles,
Not blemish'd with the stain of any breach;
Chiefly where fealty and homage willeth it.

K. James. Brother of England, rub not the sore afresh;
My conscience grieves me for my deep misdeed.
I have the worst; of thirty thousand men,
There 'scap'd not full five thousand from the field.

K. Edw. Gramercy, Musgrove, else it had gone hard:
Cuddy, I'll quite thee well ere we two part.

K. James. But had not his old father, William Musgrove,
Play'd twice the man, I had not now been here.
A stronger man I seldom felt before;
But one of more resolute valiance,
Treads not, I think, upon the English ground.

K. Edw. I wot well, Musgrove shall not lose his hire.

Cud, An it please your grace, my father was
Five-score and three at midsummer last past:
Yet had King Jamy been as good as George-a-Greene,
Yet Billy Musgrove would have fought with him.

K. Edw. As George-a-Greene!
I pray thee, Cuddy, let me question thee.
Much have I heard, since I came to my crown,
Many in manner of a proverb say,
"Were he as good as George-a-Greene, I would strike him sure:"
I pray thee, tell me, Cuddy, canst thou inform me,
What is that George-a-Greene?

Cud. Know, my lord, I never saw the man,
But mickle talk is of him in the country:
They say he is the Pinner of Wakefield town:
But for his other qualities, I let alone.

War. May it please your grace, I know the man too well.

K. Edw. Too well! why so, Warwick?

War. For once he swing'd me till my bones did ache.

K. Edw. Why, dares he strike an earl?

War. An earl, my lord! nay, he will strike a king,
Be it not King Edward. For stature he is fram'd
Like to the picture of stout Hercules,
And for his carriage passeth Robin Hood.
The boldest earl or baron of your land,
That offereth scath unto the town of Wakefield,
George will arrest his pledge unto the pound;
And whoso resisteth bears away the blows,
For he himself is good enough for three.

K. Edw. Why, this is wondrous: my Lord of Warwick,
Sore do I long to see this George-a-Greene.
But leaving him, what shall we do, my lord,
For to subdue the rebels in the north?
They are now marching up to Doncaster.—

   Enter one with the Earl of Kendal *prisoner.*

Soft! who have we there?

Cud. Here is a traitor, the Earl of Kendal.

K. Edw. Aspiring traitor! how darest thou
Once cast thine eyes upon thy sovereign
That honour'd thee with kindness, and with favour?
But I will make thee buy this treason dear.

Ken. Good my lord,—

K. Edw. Reply not, traitor.—
Tell me, Cuddy, whose deed of honour
Won the victory against this rebel?

Cud. George-a-Greene, the Pinner of Wakefield.

K. Edw. George-a-Greene! now shall I hear news
Certain, what this Pinner is.
Discourse it briefly, Cuddy, how it befell.

Cud. Kendal and Bonfield, with Sir Gilbert Armstrong,
Came to Wakefield town disguis'd,
And there spoke ill of your grace;
Which George but hearing, fell'd them at his feet,
And, had not rescue come into the place,
George had slain them in his close of wheat.

K. Edw. But, Cuddy,
Canst thou not tell where I might give and grant
Something that might please
And highly gratify the Pinner's thoughts?

Cud. This at their parting George did say to me:
"If the king vouchsafe of this my service,
Then, gentle Cuddy, kneel upon thy knee,
And humbly crave a boon of him for me."

K. Edw. Cuddy, what is it?

Cud. It is his will your grace would pardon them,
And let them live, although they have offended.

K. Edw. I think the man striveth to be glorious.
Well, George hath crav'd it, and it shall be granted,
Which none but he in England should have gotten.—
Live, Kendal, but as prisoner,
So shalt thou end thy days within the Tower.

Ken. Gracious is Edward to offending subjects.

K. James. My Lord of Kendal, you're welcome to the court.

K. Edw. Nay, but ill-come as it falls out now;

Ay, ill-come indeed, were't not for George-a-Greene.
But, gentle king, for so you would aver,
And Edward's betters, I salute you both,
And here I vow by good Saint George,
You'll gain but little when your sums are counted.
I sore do long to see this George-a-Greene:
And for because I never saw the north,
I will forthwith go see it;
And for that to none I will be known, we will
Disguise ourselves and steal down secretly,
Thou and I, King James, Cuddy, and two or three,
And make a merry journey for a month.—
Away, then, conduct him to the Tower.—
Come on, King James, my heart must needs be merry,
If fortune makes such havoc of our foes. [*Exeunt.*

SCENE II.—Robin Hood's *Retreat.*

Enter Robin Hood, Maid Marian, Scarlet, *and* Much.

Rob. Why is not lovely Marian blithe of cheer?
What ails my leman,[12] that she gins to lour?
Say, good Marian, why art thou so sad?

Mar. Nothing, my Robin, grieves me to the heart
But, whensoever I do walk abroad,
I hear no songs but all of George-a-Greene;
Bettris, his fair leman, passeth me:
And this, my Robin, galls my very soul.

Rob. Content: what recks it us though George-a-Greene be stout,
So long as he doth proffer us no scath?
Envy doth seldom hurt but to itself;
And therefore, Marian, smile upon thy Robin.

Mar. Never will Marian smile upon her Robin,
Nor lie with him under the greenwood shade,
Till that thou go to Wakefield on a green,
And beat the Pinner for the love of me.

Rob. Content thee, Marian, I will ease thy grief,
My merry men and I will thither stray;

---
[12]Love.

And here I vow that, for the love of thee,
I will beat George-a-Greene, or he shall beat me.

Scar. As I am Scarlet, next to Little John,
One of the boldest yeomen of the crew,
So will I wend with Robin all along,
And try this Pinner what he dares do.

Much. As I am Much, the miller's son,
That left my mill to go with thee,
And nill repent that I have done,
This pleasant life contenteth me;
In aught I may, to do thee good,
I'll live and die with Robin Hood.

Mar. And, Robin, Marian she will go with thee,
To see fair Bettris how bright she is of blee.[13]

Rob. Marian, thou shalt go with thy Robin.—
Bend up your bows, and see your strings be tight,
The arrows keen, and everything be ready,
And each of you a good bat on his neck,
Able to lay a good man on the ground.

Scar. I will have Friar Tuck's.

Much. I will have Little John's.

Rob. I will have one made of an ashen plank,
Able to bear a bout or two.—
Then come on, Marian, let us go;
For before the sun doth show the morning day,
I will be at Wakefield to see this Pinner, George-a-Greene.
[*Exeunt.*

SCENE III.—*At Bradford.*

A Shoemaker *discovered at work: enter* JENKIN, *carrying a staff.*[14]

Jen. My masters, he that hath neither meat nor money, and hath lost his credit with the alewife, for anything I know, may go supperless to bed.

---

[13] Colour, complexion.

[14] The stage direction in the quarto is: Enter a Shoemaker sitting upon the stage at work: Jenkin to him.

—But, soft! who is here? here is a shoemaker; he knows where is the best ale.—Shoemaker, I pray thee tell me, where is the best ale in the town?

Shoe. Afore, afore, follow thy nose; at the sign of the Egg-shell.

Jen. Come, shoemaker, if thou wilt, and take thy part of a pot.

Shoe. [*coming forward*]. Sirrah, down with your staff, down with your staff.

Jen. Why, how now! is the fellow mad? I pray thee tell me, why should I hold down my staff?

Shoe. You will down with him, will you not, sir?

Jen. Why, tell me wherefore?

Shoe. My friend, this is the town of merry Bradford, and here is a custom held, that none shall pass with his staff on his shoulders but he must have a bout with me; and so shall you, sir.

Jen. And so will I not, sir.

Shoe. That will I try. Barking dogs bite not the sorest.

Jen. [*aside*]. I would to God I were once well rid of him.

Shoe. Now, what, will you down with your staff?

Jen. Why, you are not in earnest? are you?

Shoe. If I am not, take that. [*Strikes him.*

Jen. You whoreson, cowardly scab, it is but the part of a clapperdudgeon[15] to strike a man in the street. But darest thou walk to the town's end with me?

Shoe. Ay, that I dare do; but stay till I lay in my tools, and I will go with thee to the town's end presently.

Jen. [*aside*]. I would I knew how to be rid of this fellow.

Shoe. Come, sir, will you go to the town's end now, sir?

Jen. Ay, sir, come.—

---

[15]Beggar.

[*Scene changes to the town's end*].

Now we are at the town's end, what say you now?

Shoe. Marry, come, let us even have a bout.

Jen. Ha, stay a little; hold thy hands, I pray thee.

Shoe. Why, what's the matter?

Jen. Faith, I am Under-pinner of a town, and there is an order, which if I do not keep, I shall be turned out of mine office.

Shoe. What is that, sir?

Jen. Whensoever I go to fight with anybody, I use to flourish my staff thrice about my head before I strike, and then show no favour.

Shoe. Well, sir, and till then I will not strike thee.

Jen. Well, sir, here is once, twice:—here is my hand, I will never do it the third time.

Shoe. Why, then, I see we shall not fight.

Jen. Faith, no: come, I will give thee two pots of the best ale, and be friends.

Shoe. [*aside*]. Faith, I see it is as hard to get water out of a flint as to get him to have a bout with me: therefore I will enter into him for some good cheer.—My friend, I see thou art a faint-hearted fellow, thou hast no stomach to fight, therefore let us go to the ale-house and drink.

Jen. Well, content: go thy ways, and say thy prayers, thou 'scapest my hands to-day. [*Exeunt.*

SCENE IV.—*At Wakefield.*

Enter GEORGE-A-GREENE *and* BETTRIS.

Geo. Tell me, sweet love, how is thy mind content?
What, canst thou brook to live with George-a-Greene?

Bet. O, George, how little pleasing are these words!
Came I from Bradford for the love of thee,
And left my father for so sweet a friend?
Here will I live until my life do end.

Geo. Happy am I to have so sweet a love.—
But what are these come tracing here along?

Bet. Three men come striking through the corn, my love.

   Enter Robin Hood, Maid Marian, Scarlet *and* Much.

Geo. Back again, you foolish travellers,
For you are wrong, and may not wend this way.

Rob. That were great shame. Now, by my soul, proud sir,
We be three tall[16] yeomen, and thou art but one.—
Come, we will forward in despite of him.

Geo. Leap the ditch, or I will make you skip.
What, cannot the highway serve your turn,
But you must make a path over the corn?

Rob. Why, art thou mad? dar'st thou encounter three?
We are no babes, man, look upon our limbs.

Geo. Sirrah, the biggest limbs have not the stoutest hearts.
Were ye as good as Robin Hood and his three merry men,
I'll drive you back the same way that ye came.
Be ye men, ye scorn to encounter me all at once;
But be ye cowards, set upon me all three,
And try the Pinner what he dares perform.

Scar. Were thou as high in deeds
As thou art haughty in words,
Thou well might'st be a champion for the king:
But empty vessels have the loudest sounds,
And cowards prattle more than men of worth.

Geo. Sirrah, darest thou try me?

Scar. Ay, sirrah, that I dare.
[*They fight, and* George-a-Greene *beats him.*

Much. How now! what, art thou down?—
Come, sir, I am next.

---

[16]Bold, brave.

[*They fight, and* George-a-Greene *beats him.*

Rob. Come, sirrah, now to me: spare me not,
For I'll not spare thee.

Ge. Make no doubt I will be as liberal to thee.
[*They fight*; Robin Hood *stays.*

Rob. Stay, George, for here I do protest,
Thou art the stoutest champion that ever I
Laid hands upon.

Geo. Soft, you sir! by your leave, you lie;
You never yet laid hands on me.

Rob. George, wilt thou forsake Wakefield,
And go with me?
Two liveries will I give thee every year,
And forty crowns shall be thy fee.[17]

Geo. Why, who art thou?

Rob. Why, Robin Hood:
I am come hither with my Marian
And these my yeomen for to visit thee.

Geo. Robin Hood!
Next to King Edward art thou lief[18] to me.
Welcome, sweet Robin; welcome, Maid Marian;
And welcome, you my friends. Will you to my poor house?
You shall have wafer-cakes your fill,
A piece of beef hung up since Martlemas,
Mutton and veal: if this like you not,
Take that you find, or that you bring, for me.

Rob. Godamercies, good George,
I'll be thy guest to-day.

Geo. Robin, therein thou honourest me.
I'll lead the way. [*Exeunt.*

---

[17] See the ballad printed in the Appendix.
[18] Dear.

ACT V.

SCENE I.—*At Bradford.*

Enter KING EDWARD *and* KING JAMES *disguised; each carrying a staff.*

K. Edw. Come on, King James; now we are thus disguis'd,
There's none, I know, will take us to be kings:
I think we are now in Bradford,
Where all the merry shoemakers dwell.

Enter several Shoemakers.

First Shoe. Down with your staves, my friends,
Down with them.

K. Edw. Down with our staves! I pray thee, why so?

First Shoe. My friend, I see thou art a stranger here,
Else wouldst thou not have question'd of the thing.
This is the town of merry Bradford,
And here hath been a custom kept of old,
That none may bear his staff upon his neck,
But trail it all along throughout the town,
Unless they mean to have a bout with me.

K. Edw. But hear you, sir, hath the king granted you this custom?

First Shoe. King or kaisar, none shall pass this way,
Except King Edward;
No, not the stoutest groom that haunts his court;
Therefore down with your staves.

K. Edw. What were we best to do?

K. James. Faith, my lord, they are stout fellows;
And, because we will see some sport,
We will trail our staves.

K. Edw. Hear'st thou, my friend?
Because we are men of peace and travellers,
We are content to trail our staves.

First Shoe. The way lies before you, go along.

Enter Robin Hood *and* George-a-Greene, *disguised.*

Rob. See, George, two men are passing through the town,
Two lusty men, and yet they trail their staves.

Geo. Robin, they are some peasants trick'd in yeoman's weeds.—
Hollo, you two travellers!

K. Edw. Call you us, sir?

Geo. Ay, you. Are ye not big enough to bear
Your bats upon your necks, but you must trail them
Along the streets?

K. Edw. Yes, sir, we are big enough; but here is a custom kept,
That none may pass, his staff upon his neck,
Unless he trail it at the weapon's point.
Sir, we are men of peace, and love to sleep
In our whole skins, and therefore quietness is best.

Geo. Base-minded peasants, worthless to be men!
What, have you bones and limbs to strike a blow,
And be your hearts so faint you cannot fight?
Were't not for shame, I would drub your shoulders well,
And teach you manhood 'gainst another time.

First Shoe. Well preach'd, Sir Jack! down with your staff!

K. Edw. Do you hear, my friends? an you be wise, keep down
Your staves, for all the town will rise upon you.

Geo. Thou speakest like an honest, quiet fellow:
But hear you me; in spite of all the swains
Of Bradford town, bear me your staves upon your necks,
Or, to begin withal, I'll baste you both so well,
You were never better basted in your lives.

K. Edw. We will hold up our staves.
[George-a-Greene *fights with the* Shoemakers, *and beats them all down.*

Geo. What, have you any more?
Call all your town forth, cut and longtail.[19]

---
[19]Derived first from the language of the chase, this phrase probably came to mean "dogs of all kinds."

[*The* Shoemakers *recognise* George-a-Greene.

First Shoe. What, George a-Greene, is it you? A plague found[20] you!
I think you long'd to swinge me well.
Come, George, we will crush a pot before we part.

Geo. A pot, you slave! we will have an hundred.—
Here, Will Perkins, take my purse; fetch me
A stand of ale, and set in the market-place,
That all may drink that are athirst this day;
For this is for a fee to welcome Robin Hood
To Bradford town.
[*The stand of ale is brought out, and they fall a-drinking.*
Here, Robin, sit thou here;
For thou art the best man at the board this day.
You that are strangers, place yourselves where you will.
Robin, here's a carouse to good King Edward's self;
And they that love him not, I would we had
The basting of them a little.

Enter the Earl of Warwick *with other* Noblemen, *bringing out the* King's *garments; then* George-a-Greene *and the rest kneel down to the* King.

K. Edw. Come, masters, ale—fellows.—Nay, Robin,
You are the best man at the board to-day.—
Rise up, George.

Geo. Nay, good my liege, ill-nurtur'd we were, then:
Though we Yorkshire men be blunt of speech,
And little skill'd in court or such quaint fashions,
Yet nature teacheth us duty to our king;
Therefore I humbly beseech you pardon George-a-Greene.

Rob. And, good my lord, a pardon for poor Robin;
And for us all a pardon, good King Edward.

First Shoe. I pray you, a pardon for the shoemakers.

K. Edw. I frankly grant a pardon to you all:
[*They rise.*
And, George-a-Greene, give me thy hand;

---
[20]Confound.

There's none in England that shall do thee wrong.
Even from my court I came to see thyself;
And now I see that fame speaks naught but truth.

Geo. I humbly thank your royal majesty.
That which I did against the Earl of Kendal,
'Twas but a subject's duty to his sovereign,
And therefore little merits such good words.

K. Edw. But ere I go, I'll grace thee with good deeds.
Say what King Edward may perform,
And thou shalt have it, being in England's bounds.

Geo. I have a lovely leman,
As bright of blee as is the silver moon,
And old Grime her father will not let her match
With me, because I am a Pinner,
Although I love her, and she me, dearly.

K. Edw. Where is she?

Geo. At home at my poor house,
And vows never to marry unless her father
Give consent; which is my great grief, my lord.

K. Edw. If this be all, I will despatch it straight;
I'll send for Grime and force him give his grant:
He will not deny King Edward such a suit.

Enter JENKIN.

Jen. Ho, who saw a master of mine? O, he is gotten into company, an a body should rake hell for company.

Geo. Peace, ye slave! see where King Edward is.

K. Edw. George, what is he?

Geo. I beseech your grace pardon him; he is my man.

First Shoe. Sirrah, the king hath been drinking with us, and did pledge us too.

Jen. Hath he so? kneel; I dub you gentlemen.

First Shoe. Beg it of the king, Jenkin.

Jen. I will.—I beseech your worship grant me one thing.

K. Edw. What is that?

Jen. Hark in your ear. [*Whispers* K. EDW. *in the ear.*

K. Edw. Go your ways, and do it.

Jen. Come, down on your knees, I have got it.

First Shoe. Let us hear what it is first.

Jen. Marry, because you have drunk with the king, and the king hath so graciously pledged you, you shall be no more called Shoemakers; but you and yours, to the world's end, shall be called the trade of the Gentle Craft.

First Shoe. I beseech your majesty reform this which he hath spoken.

Jen. I beseech your worship consume this which he hath spoken.

K. Edw. Confirm it, you would say.—
Well, he hath done it for you, it is sufficient.—
Come, George, we will go to Grime, and have thy love.

Jen. I am sure your worship will abide; for yonder is coming old Musgrove and mad Cuddy his son.—Master, my fellow Wily comes dressed like a woman, and Master Grime will marry Wily. Here they come.

    Enter MUSGROVE *and* CUDDY; GRIME, WILY *disguised as a woman,* MAID MARIAN, *and* BETTRIS.

K. Edw. Which is thy old father, Cuddy?

Cud. This, if it please your majesty.
[MUSGROVE *kneels.*

K. Edw. Ah, old Musgrove, stand up;
It fits not such grey hairs to kneel.

Mus. [*rising*]. Long live my sovereign!
Long and happy be his days!
Vouchsafe, my gracious lord, a simple gift

At Billy Musgrove's hand.
King James at Middleham Castle gave me this;
This won the honour, and this give I thee.
[*Gives sword to* K. EDW.

K. Edw. Godamercy, Musgrove, for this friendly gift;
And, for thou fell'dst a king with this same weapon,
This blade shall here dub valiant Musgrove knight.

Mus. Alas, what hath your highness done? I am poor.

K. Edw. To mend thy living take thou Middleham Castle,
And hold of me. And if thou want living, complain;
Thou shalt have more to maintain thine estate.—
George, which is thy love?

Geo. This, if please your majesty.

K. Edw. Art thou her aged father?

Grime. I am, an it like your majesty.

K. Edw. And wilt not give thy daughter unto George?

Grime. Yes, my lord, if he will let me marry with this lovely lass.

K. Edw. What say'st thou, George?

Geo. With all my heart, my lord, I give consent.

Grime. Then do I give my daughter unto George.

Wily. Then shall the marriage soon be at an end.
Witness, my lord, if that I be a woman;
[*Throws off his disguise.*
For I am Wily, boy to George-a-Greene,
Who for my master wrought this subtle shift.

K. Edw. What, is it a boy?—what say'st thou to this, Grime?

Grime. Marry, my lord, I think this boy hath
More knavery than all the world besides.
Yet am I content that George shall both have
My daughter and my lands.

K. Edw. Now, George, it rests I gratify thy worth:
And therefore here I do bequeath to thee,
In full possession, half that Kendal hath;
And what as Bradford holds of me in chief,
I give it frankly unto thee for ever.
Kneel down, George.

Geo. What will your majesty do?

K. Edw. Dub thee a knight, George.

Geo. I beseech your grace, grant me one thing.

K. Edw. What is that?

Geo. Then let me live and die a yeoman still:
So was my father, so must live his son.
For 'tis more credit to men of base degree,
To do great deeds, than men of dignity.

K. Edw. Well, be it so, George.

K. James. I beseech your grace despatch with me,
And set down my ransom.

K. Edw. George-a-Greene,
Set down the King of Scots his ransom.

Geo. I beseech your grace pardon me;
It passeth my skill.

K. Edw. Do it, the honour's thine.

Geo. Then let King James make good
Those towns which he hath burnt upon the borders;
Give a small pension to the fatherless,
Whose fathers he caus'd murder'd in those wars;
Put in pledge for these things to your grace,
And so return.

K. Edw. King James, are you content?

K. James. I am content, an like your majesty,

And will leave good castles in security.

K. Edw. I crave no more.—Now, George-a-Greene,
I'll to thy house; and when I have supt, I'll go
To ask and see if Jane-a-Barley be so fair
As good King James reports her for to be.
And for the ancient custom of *Vail staff,*
Keep it still, claim privilege from me:
If any ask a reason why, or how,
Say, English Edward vail'd his staff to you.
[*Exeunt omnes.*

APPENDIX

THE JOLLY PINDER OF WAKEFIELD
WITH ROBIN HOOD, SCARLET AND JOHN.

In Wakefield there lives a jolly pindèr,
in Wakefield all on a green,
in Wakefield all on a green;

There is neither knight nor squire, said the pindèr,
nor baron that is so bold,
nor baron that is so bold;

Dare make a trespàss to the town of Wakefield,
but his pledge goes to the pinfold, &c.

All this be heard three witty young men,
'twas Robin Hood, Scarlet and John, &c.

With that they espy'd the jolly pindèr,
as he sat under a thorn, &c.

Now turn again, turn again, said the pindèr,
for a wrong way you have gone, &c.

For you have forsaken the king's high-way,
and made a path over the corn, &c.

O that were great shame, said jolly Robin,
we being three, and thou but one, &c.

The pinder leapt back then thirty good foot,
'twas thirty good foot and one, &c.

He leaned his back fast unto a thorn,
and his foot against a stone, &c.

And there they fought a long summer's day,
a summer's day so long, &c.

Till that their swords on their broad bucklèrs,
were broke fast into their hands, &c.

Hold thy hand, hold thy hand, said bold Robin Hood,
and my merry men everyone, &c.

For this is one of the best pindèrs,
that ever I tryed with sword, &c.

And wilt thou forsake thy pinder's craft,
and live in the green-wood with me? &c.

At Michaelmas next my cov'nant comes out,
when every man gathers his fee, &c.

I'll take my blew blade all in my hand
And plod to the green-wood with thee, &c.

Hast thou either meat or drink? said Robin Hood,
for my merry men and me, &c.

I have both bread and beef, said the pindèr,
and good ale of the best, &c.

And that is meat good enough, said Robin Hood,
for such unbidden guest, &c.

O wilt thou forsake the pinder his craft,
and go to the green-wood with me? &c.

Thou shalt have a livery twice in the year,
the one green, the other brown, &c.

If Michaelmas day was come and gone,
and my master had paid me my fee,
and my master had paid me my fee,

Then would I set as little by him,
as my master doth by me,
as my master doth by me.

Made in the USA
Coppell, TX
28 May 2021